Out of Control:

A Guide to Navigating Unsafe Relationships

Recognize manipulation, reclaim your peace, and safely plan your way out.

Marie Jones

Table of Contents

Introduction

This book is a personal guide for anyone who suspects they may be in an unsafe, emotionally or physically abusive relationship. It is my hope that this guide will help you recognize the signs of abuse, understand the psychological manipulation that keeps people stuck, and give you practical tools to help you begin to find clarity, safety, and eventually freedom. You are not alone, and there is a way out.

The purpose of this book is to help you better understand what this type of abuse looks like. I pray that, equipped with tools and knowledge, you might be able to find peace and freedom as well.

Before we get started, I would like to share a few insights with you regarding the way this book was written. This book is written by a survivor of abuse. Me. As a survivor, there are a couple of things that I would have wanted if I were ever back in an unsafe situation.

First, I have purposefully made this book short, simple, and hopefully easy to understand. I recognize that in abusive relationships, we often do not have the luxury of time to process information. If you are in one of these relationships, you are in survival mode. It's common and normal that your brain space is most occupied with just that, survival. I have also purposefully omitted as much from the title as possible for the reader to understand the purpose, without a title that screams I WANT TO GET AWAY FROM YOU. I hope that by doing this, you may have some extra time to explore what it means to leave unsafe relationships.

Also, while I do have extensive experience in my personal career with personality disorders as well as the diagnosis of other mental health conditions, I am not a clinician. Because of this, the book will be written from my experience and by omitting clinical labels such as Narcissistic and Antisocial Personality Disorder. While this would most likely be the clinical diagnosis for the type of behavior we are discussing, some abusers do not have this diagnosis. I will let you do your research and form your own opinion. For this book, I have used the term, unsafe relationships. Because that is what it is. Unsafe. Believe it and know it down in your soul. We need to escape from unsafe people.

It is important to remember that even without these labels, the behavior is exactly the same. It is the same whether you are male or female, and I want to make it clear, this book is for EVERYONE who needs it. Unsafe relationships can happen to anyone, not just women.

I want you to hear this from the bottom of my heart. Even if it wasn't physical, it is still physical. The difference with physical intimidation is the immediacy of a direct threat to your life. Aside from that horror, the feeling is familiar to all of us who have been affected. It happens to ALL people, but most often the best of the best. They aren't going to hang on to a loser. You have a spark, a glow about you. It's so bright that they want to dim it. Don't let them.

A Final Word Before We Start

This statement might go against conventional wisdom, but I want to make this clear as you are reading this book and making plans:

You need to do what you have to do to survive and escape the situation safely. This means there may be times when you really can't afford to fight back because of the danger it could pose to you. To safely escape, you must be clever and keep a calm demeanor so that you can think clearly. Remember the long game. Safety.

This often goes against the conventional advice of others who are giving advice based on their experience with "normal" human beings. In a healthy relationship, you might be advised to sit down with the person, tell them your concerns. They might even suggest that you need to firmly set down boundaries, expressing your anger calmly. Keep in mind, they are anything but normal. Advice for normal people is not always going to work. It may not be safe to give them a piece of your mind. Take each piece of advice with a grain of salt. You know them best, don't tempt fate.

You can't love them enough to heal them. You can't fight your way into being respected. Injuries to their ego can be dangerous.

So, your first and only priority has to be your safety.

Some days, that might mean walking on eggshells to survive the night. Some days, that might mean staying quiet, not fighting back, even when every part of you wants to scream.

I used to fantasize about pushing him right back. I wanted justice. I wanted revenge.

But more than anything, I wanted to live. I knew one aggressive move on my part, and I was done. He had superhuman strength during those times. Everything in me screamed, screw you, dude. But I had to play it safe.

So, I kept my head down, made a plan, and waited until I could get out.

Be safe while you make your plan.

Don't judge yourself for doing what it takes to survive.

You're not weak, you are resourceful.

You are kind, brilliant, and compassionate.

I wrote this book for you.

And you are not alone.

Chapter 1
The Spin Begins

I remember the day we met so vividly. Something was different about him, I thought. Different but in a good way. I remember the intense feeling of being wanted and loved, almost as if it were the first time. Whereas others might have piddled around, hesitating before holding my hand, hesitating before going straight in for the first kiss, not him. It wasn't like me to move so fast, but his infatuation with my every move kept me hooked. He wouldn't take no for an answer when I told him we should take it slow, but he couldn't stand the thought of losing the perfect woman for him, so that was okay, right? At last, someone finally saw my worth. Everything about him dripped with perfection. He listened to my stories, he empathized, and he was incensed by past mistreatments. How dare they treat me this way, not now, not under his watch. He met my daughter, a preteen at the time, and quickly assumed a self-appointed position as family patriarch. For me, it felt good to finally have someone as a partner, to support me as I navigated life's challenges.

At first, his gestures were grand, his love was larger than life. It felt like a movie. I had found my perfect romance. I had found him. Love at first sight is what we told people. And oh, how we could laugh! People who had known me for years sent congratulations; they had never seen me so happy. They had never seen me smile in this way. He, nearly perfect, aside from some misfortunes that had fallen on him through no fault of his own, had been sent from heaven. In fact, I prayed for him. I proudly told him this on our second date. I had made a list, I told him. He checked each box miraculously.

A quick engagement ensued. Although much of the façade had begun to fade, I wanted to be married. All of the dating books I read pushed the idea that without marriage, you might be faced with years of being strung along just to ultimately be left by another woman who checked more of the imaginary boxes than me. I didn't want that for sure. Despite the mounting red flags, I remember looking down at my sparkling new engagement ring with pride. I would be checking off that long-awaited box. I would not be that woman. Marriage and then babies would come quickly, I thought. What a perfect life.

On my wedding day, I was granted a reprieve from the nagging fear that it was all wrong. He smiled, he danced, he kissed me at the appropriate times, he shook my parents' hands, promising that he would be there to take care of me for the rest of my life. I had hope that marriage would reestablish the respect he had for me. The good times had felt so good that I would do anything to make this newly found pain stop. In his brief and fleeting moments of kindness, I felt a sense of relief; these now rare moments were so coveted that I would do anything to grant myself even a moment of relief. Anything. It had become markedly less perfect for sure, but with enough love and hard work, we could overcome everything. Just like he said at the beginning.

Except it wasn't like the beginning at all now. Those quirks about me that he loved at the beginning now seemed to make me a target. Gone was the kind, benevolent soul, with boundless patience and unconditional love. The hands that had once held me seemed to harden, like his now constantly disdainful demeanor. I did my best to push away the concerns and nagging premonition that things might not turn out okay like I thought. He began to shatter my confidence, reserving the worst cruelty for nighttime hours, behind closed doors. I would often cry late into the night, leaving my eyes puffy and swollen. In the morning, I would make excuses to coworkers for things like lack of sleep, insomnia, and allergies. Whereas I used to love the way he would joke around with me, the joking turned into shoves, a quick but painful flick on the head, his hands on my neck, an assisted, unintentional trip down the front 2 stairs that would land me on the ground. Enough that there wasn't a bruise, but there was terror.

I began to notice things about my physical appearance that extended beyond the puffy morning eyes. My face was blotched, overstressed, and even though I didn't weigh the most I ever weighed, I looked like that plus 10. Everything was sitting differently. I aged, and quickly. My skin was dull, the light also gone from my eyes, and I looked like a shadow of my former self. The glow was gone.

I was gone.

Aside from my physical appearance, my mental health was also in sharp decline. My memory was completely shot. Suddenly, whereas I used to be sharp and on top of things, I had a hard time putting simple thoughts into words, which only seemed to incense him more. My nervous system now seemed to be on a low stall, constantly running. I was exhausted. My heart would often pound for no reason. I adjusted everything in my life to accommodate him, but no effort seemed to satisfy his constantly changing standards. His anger gradually changed to include acts of terror. He thrived on the shock factor. Despite my begging for just a few minutes of reprieve, he did not grant it. I was imprisoned in every way with no escape in sight. I struggled to understand the pattern and internalized the blame. Why couldn't I get it right?!

While the bruises weren't there for the world to see, I was taking a beating. In my search to put it all together, I eventually began to stumble upon descriptions of behavior that seemed to fit his mold. Words like narcissistic abuse, complex PTSD, me antisocial personality disorder seemed to especially resonate, and more. The more I searched, the more his behavior made sense. I eventually put together tools that helped me to escape this life I had not asked for, a life that was at risk of ending mine. I found comfort in knowing others had gone through the same things that I was experiencing. Some days, it was the only light that would shine through.

Looking Back: What I Wish I Had Known

When you're in it, you can't see it. The red flags don't look red — they look like romance, like passion, like finally being chosen. But now, with distance and clarity, I can see the warning signs that were there from the very beginning. Signs I explained away, rationalized, or mistook for love. If you're reading this and something feels familiar, trust that feeling. Your intuition is trying to tell you something.

The Warning Signs I Missed

1. The intensity came too fast, too soon.

He pursued me relentlessly. When I asked to slow down, he didn't respect that boundary—he bulldozed right through it, framing it as devotion. "I can't stand the thought of losing you," he said. I heard love. What it actually was: a refusal to respect my needs from day one.

2. Overly fascinated with details regarding my past traumas.

He wanted every detail of how others had hurt me. I thought it was empathy. What it actually was: research. He was learning my vulnerabilities, cataloging my wounds so he'd know exactly where to strike later.

3. Need to perform for loved ones.

Friends who'd known me for years said they'd never seen me smile like this. I wore that like a badge of honor. What I didn't realize: I was performing happiness to justify a relationship that was already making me uneasy. I could not be honest with my loved ones for the first time and I found myself hiding or sugar coating my reality. This is a serious red flag.

4. The good times felt so good that I'd do anything to get them back.

Even as things deteriorated, those brief moments of kindness became precious, rare, something I'd sacrifice anything to experience again. What I didn't see: that's the hook. The intermittent reinforcement good, then bad, then good again — is more addictive than consistent love ever could be.

5. My concerns were dismissed and minimized.

When I tried to voice worry or discomfort, I was told I was too sensitive, too dramatic, misremembering, or overreacting. What it actually was: the beginning of erasing my reality and replacing it with his. He was constantly pushing my boundaries and ignored my unease. I always somehow found myself apologizing, even when it was absurdly his fault. This denial of reality is one of the first signs that things will one day become unsafe.

Questions to Ask Yourself

These aren't easy questions. You don't have to answer them for anyone but yourself. But if you're willing to sit with them honestly, they might illuminate something you've been trying not to see.

- Looking back at the beginning of your relationship, what felt too good to be true?
- Were there moments when you wanted to slow down, set a boundary, or pump the brakes — but didn't? What stopped you?

- Have you ever caught yourself making excuses for someone's behavior to friends, family, or yourself? What were you excusing?

Chapter 2
Waking Up to Chaos – Everything Is Not What It Seems

In living with unsafe people, the morning provides the opportunity for one of their favorite things to do. Ruin your day. It is usually in the morning or late at night that their true self comes to light.

Like most things that unsafe people do, they do it behind closed doors. And often it is not immediately obvious what they are doing because on the surface, they usually have some (halfway) legitimate complaint. Legitimate enough to make you feel a sense of shame, like you should apologize, if for no other reason than to shut them up. Sadly, the apology is never enough. They require groveling and bad news, but that isn't enough either. If you do manage to get silence, it is not in a good way. They cut you off emotionally to ensure your voice is not heard. They leave and don't return for hours or days; you pay the price either way. And I am not sure which is worse. Either way, you cry or sit there numb because you have given up. Subsequently, it ruins your day, and if it is night, it ruins your night too.

While I am sure some unsafe people turn perfectly evil midday, for the most part, the beginning and the end of the day are where you can often find your answers about the safety of your partner.

Would you never purposefully ruin the day of someone you love, right? So, what makes them do that?

This chapter is about learning to identify the tell-tale signs and symptoms of abusive relationships. It looks different for everyone, but there are some hallmarks that you can always count on.

What do unsafe relationships look like?

In unsafe relationships, the goal isn't love, it's power. It is ALL about power. Even during their angelic, getting to know you stage, it is all setting the stage for power. People with unsafe behaviors often seek control, admiration, and compliance. They don't build relationships based on mutual respect; they build them like traps. All the getting to know you, the moments of vulnerability, the sharing of intimate details, it is a trap. Even if they might deny it emphatically at the time, it will eventually come into play.

Common signs of Unsafe People include:

- Constant criticism, mockery, or subtle put-downs
- Gaslighting: denying your reality, twisting facts, making you question yourself
- Isolation from friends, family, or outside support
- Sudden shifts between idealizing you and devaluing you
- Using affection, attention, or money as tools of control
- Never taking responsibility; everything becomes your fault

If you're constantly wondering, "Am I overreacting?" or "Why do I feel like I'm going crazy?" those are huge red flags. Healthy relationships don't leave you in a constant state of self-doubt or fear.

I know for me personally, I spent hours and hours scrolling through narcissistic abuse pages, reading books, doing internet searches to try my best to understand what was happening to me. I would search high and low for signs that could help me understand, to assure me that I wasn't the bad person.

Now, I know that this is not normal. If you have to go out of your way to understand them and tie your brain all up into a pretzel trying to figure things out, that is a huge red flag. Safe people don't require all this effort. Of course, they will mess up from time to time because that is human. But there are normal, genuine mistakes people make, and then there are mistakes that completely disregard your humanity. If you are searching and praying to make sense of it all, that is not healthy, and it is a sign to get out.

Why It's So Hard to See?

People often ask, "Why didn't you just leave?" or my favorite, "I would never put up with that."

But when you're inside an emotionally abusive relationship, it's not that simple.

- You're always chasing the good times. The highs feel intoxicating, and the lows feel devastating, but you're hooked on the cycle.
- You're isolated. The abuser often cuts you off from people who might challenge their control.
- You lose trust in yourself. Over time, you stop trusting your own instincts.

- You still love them. And they use that love as leverage.

Abuse isn't a constant punch in the face. It's a slow erosion of self, mixed with just enough kindness to keep you hoping they'll change.

One thing that I think is important to point out is that most controlling, unsafe people are not ALWAYS bad. This can be tricky for our minds. You could have one of the most awful days of your life with them, but in the end, they hug you and thank you for sticking around. They say they are sorry and make you feel loved and adored for just a moment. This is not genuine kindness.

Something that I have had to tell myself over and over, even years later, is that they don't think the same way as we do. The things that we do, that normal people do, usually do not resonate with them. There could be many reasons for these moments of sanity. Some might feel a temporary tinge of guilt; some might want to ensure you stay around for their own benefit. Sometimes they need a roof over their head or a free meal. Sometimes they are just bored that day and want to see how much they can get you upset and flustered. For them, this behavior is a big dopamine hit. They get high from the control and the power. And some just do it for the hell of it. Just to be mean.

Unsafe people are just that, mean.

What Helped Me Wake Up

What helped me was information and validation. The day I read a list of commonly used abuse tactics and saw my life written out in black and white, I cried with relief. It was real. I wasn't imagining it. I wasn't broken; I was being broken down. I found lots of comfort listening to people's stories. I found infinite comfort in the many advocates on social media who bring awareness to these topics. I watched these videos over and over. Understanding it brought me some peace.

If you're reading this and some part of you is whispering, "This feels familiar," please listen to that voice. It's not paranoia. It's your intuition trying to get your attention.

Tools to Get Clear

You don't need to diagnose your partner or prove they have a disorder. What matters is how the relationship makes you feel.

Here are a few simple tools to start sorting out truth from confusion:

1. The "Would I Say This to a Friend?" Test

Think of something your partner says or does often. Now ask yourself: if a friend told you their partner did that to them, would you think it was okay?

If your immediate reaction is "Oh God, no, I'd tell her to run," but you're staying put yourself—pay attention to that disconnect. You deserve the same care and concern you'd give a friend.

2. *Keep a Private Journal (or Voice Notes)*

Record what happens: dates, conversations, how you felt. When you're being gaslit, this record becomes your anchor to reality.

But here's the key: Don't just write what happened. Use a structure that helps you see patterns and cut through the confusion they create.

Simple Journal Template:

Date/Time:

What happened (just the facts):

Write it like you're describing a scene in a movie. No interpretation, no emotion yet—just what was said and done.

Important: Keep this journal somewhere they cannot access it. A password-protected note on your phone, a private Google doc, a notebook hidden at work or at a trusted friend's house. If they find it, they will use it against you.

3. The "Video Test"

Here's a quick reality check that cuts through gaslighting instantly:

Ask yourself: "If someone had filmed this moment, what would the video show?"

Not what he says happened. Not what you're afraid you did wrong. What would an objective recording show?

Would it show you "screaming and losing it," or would it show you speaking firmly while he talks over you and then accuses you of yelling?

Would it show you "starting a fight," or would it show you asking a simple question that he exploded over?

The video doesn't lie. And if the video shows something completely different than what he's claiming, you're being gaslit.

4. Use the Word "Safe" Instead of "Good"

Don't ask "Is this relationship good?" Ask, "Do I feel emotionally safe here?"

Safety is the foundation. Without it, nothing else works.

A relationship can have good moments, great sex, fun vacations, shared interests — and still be deeply unsafe. Don't let the occasional highs distract you from the constant baseline of fear, walking on eggshells, and self-censoring.

5. *Listen to Your Body*

Sometimes your body knows before your mind is ready to accept it.

Your nervous system is trying to tell you something. If you're experiencing any of these physical symptoms regularly, pay attention:

- Jaw clenching or teeth grinding, especially at night or when you hear them come home
- Stomach problems—nausea, digestive issues, loss of appetite, or stress eating
- Trouble sleeping—insomnia, nightmares, waking up in a panic, or sleeping too much to escape
- Constant muscle tension, especially in your neck, shoulders, or back
- Heart racing or pounding for no apparent reason, or feeling like you can't catch your breath
- Frequent headaches or migraines
- Getting sick more often—your immune system is compromised by chronic stress
- Feeling frozen or numb, like you're watching your life happen to someone else

These aren't just stress. This is your body in survival mode. If your body is sending you these signals, believe it. Your nervous system doesn't lie.

Why These Tools Matter

These aren't just exercises. They're lifelines.

When you're being told that your reality isn't real, that your feelings are wrong, that you're too sensitive or too dramatic or too broken—these tools give you something solid to hold onto. They give you proof.

Use them. Come back to them when you're doubting yourself. And if you're not ready to leave yet, that's okay—but start documenting. Start paying attention. Start listening to the part of you that knows something is very, very wrong.

Quick Chapter Summary

- Abuse can be invisible- especially emotional or psychological.
- Narcissistic and antisocial partners use charm, gaslighting, and control.
- If you feel unsafe, confused, or like you're always walking on eggshells, it's a sign that something is wrong.
- You are not imagining it. Trust the part of you that's questioning the chaos.

Chapter 3
Losing Yourself – How Unsafe Relationships Erode Identity

Back in my teen years, I could have only been described as an overachieving extrovert. If there was a social event, I was there. Not only was I there, but I was also likely to have been organizing it. I was consistently the center of attention, a hub of creativity and academic achievement, motivated, optimistic, and dreaming of a future where I would one day be a great leader, maybe a politician or governor. I felt as if I was going somewhere.

This drive that I had continued into college, where I added majors and minors quickly to get where I had dreamed in life. I was a writer for the university newspaper, I was the president of the student council, and I played intramural sports. And of course, no time was spared for parties, football games, tailgates, or anything to have a good time. I gathered up awards, a bachelor's degree, and even added a master's degree when it was all said and done. After graduation, I built a successful career in the mental health field. I felt equipped in this role and spent many years working with those struggling with their mental health, as well as situations just like mine.

I met my husband in my late 30s, feeling the pressure to get married. Like most first dates, we spent it talking about our lives. He was impressed by my professional role and even bragged to others about all that I had accomplished. I was impressed by his attentiveness as he got to know me. He seemed focused on my successes, and he went out of his way to impress the family and friends I had gathered over the years. I was so happy; I was on cloud nine. Life was good.

Fast forward 5 years, and that same woman was nowhere to be found. I noticed that the joy had left my life, and it was replaced by a constant sense of dread. My system was constantly on edge, and panic attacks became an everyday occurrence. If I could manage a smile, it seemed more for survival than any kind of joy. While he called it laziness, I had difficulty gaining motivation. After all, what was the point of keeping up my appearance, keeping the house clean, what was the point of cooking? What was the point of even getting up? Nothing was good enough, and nothing would ever be good enough.

I realized I no longer made simple decisions without fear. Most of my days were spent as someone who was desperately trying to avoid landmines. All my decisions, big or small, were vetted. I had learned how to predict his moods before he walked in the door.

Unfortunately, my daughter had too, and she was also beginning to show signs of emotional wear. After all, it must have been hard being scared for her mother, while also trying to manage her own panic and fear. The effects on both of us became marked. I avoided people and things I had always enjoyed. It was easier to avoid them than the emotional abuse I would endure by choosing a night out with my girls. Although my loved ones would be disappointed, at least it wouldn't leave me with bruises and emotional scars. Slowly but surely, he twisted my world in a flurry of pure survival, and through his incremental conditioning, I began to think it was normal.

The truth is, unsafe people don't just hurt us physically and emotionally; it requires us to adapt to survive. You may become quiet, hyper-aware, constantly scanning for danger. People often begin to confuse control for care, silence for peace, and exhaustion for safety. And after a while, you don't recognize who you are anymore.

This chapter is about that loss of self, and what is actually happening to your brain and body when you live in a constant state of emotional survival.

What is Complex PTSD?

You've probably heard of PTSD, which is usually connected to a specific traumatic event. But Complex PTSD (CPTSD) is different. It's what happens when the trauma is ongoing, subtle, and relational, like abuse from a partner, parent, or caregiver.

CPTSD symptoms often include:

- Emotional flashbacks (sudden feelings of fear, shame, or rage with no clear trigger)
- Chronic self-doubt or guilt
- People-pleasing or fawning (appeasing to avoid conflict)
- Feeling disconnected from yourself or others
- Depression, anxiety, or emotional numbness

These aren't character flaws. They're survival adaptations. Your nervous system learned how to keep you safe in an unsafe environment.

CPTSD can be incredibly impairing. Knowing (or suspecting) that you have it can help you to better understand yourself, but it often does little to change the constant, unrelenting effects on your nervous system that impact every single day of your life. My journey with CPTSD has been the most difficult part of the days and years following my abusive marriage. Often, we don't understand where our feelings are originating. For instance, something as simple as going to the grocery store would feel pretty much in line with how I would feel entering a den of lions. So many days I would sit in front of the store, my heart racing, before finally I would just drive away rather than putting myself through what used to be the simplest task.

Here are a couple of other things I noticed in myself that could be other lesser discussed effects of CPTSD. Please note that it looks different for everybody, but I am hoping that some of these might also resonate with you. Remember, one of the keys to healing is understanding and self-compassion.

- Reduced emotional tolerance: I would notice my very short tolerance for loud chaotic events. Concerts were nearly unbearable, parties with screaming children would leave me running back to my own house for days of recovery. I would notice that even things I had always enjoyed, that posed absolutely no threat to me, such as a girl's night, had a very short expiration date before I would inevitably need to go find a quiet place to sit for a while. In short, it ALL felt scary. All of it, no matter how enjoyable and innocent the event.

Random Disassociation

Something else that was very difficult was the disassociation I would experience when things got stressful. For those who don't know, dissociation is a disconnection or a detachment from one's sense of self. Does anyone remember the classic movie "A Christmas Story"? The main character, Ralphie, driven by his drive for a BB gun, would unexpectedly transport to random fantasies, finally coming back to reality after a time. In many ways, I felt like Ralphie as soon as a minor stress would occur. I would find myself drifting away. The worst part, I couldn't control it. For me, unfortunately, it often came along when I was required to give large presentations at work. For some reason, the nerves associated with that would throw me straight into fight or flight. Right before the presentation, I would suddenly feel disconnected from my body. It took everything in me to stay present enough not to make a fool out of myself. I was hypervigilant throughout. Taking questions was particularly a struggle as I would have difficulty tracking what they were asking. I was frozen.

Hypersensitivity

There were times when my boss would be giving gentle, kind constructive feedback, feedback that they would give to any employee, but for me, the slight "criticism" felt similar to my body, like the days I was being put down by my ex. For days, I would turn their comments over and over in my head, analyzing each word for signs of danger. One comment would have me running to look for a new job. I was ready to start a new career just to avoid ever answering a question again. I analyzed every single event, every statement, every email for signs of danger.

Today, I am very grateful for kind, trauma-informed bosses who did not give up on me during these early days of awkward presentations and unplanned freezes. While it is not always possible to find such a workplace during a crisis, over time, it might be useful to find a workplace that is gentle on your nervous system.

The Erosion of Identity

In controlling relationships, your identity gets rewritten over time. The person you were, your opinions, your voice, your needs, get buried under the weight of someone else's expectations.

You may hear things like:

- "You're too sensitive."
- "No one else would put up with you."
- "Why do you always ruin everything?"

After years of this, you start to internalize it. The abuser no longer has to say those words; you say them to yourself.

That's the heartbreak of abuse: it convinces you that the problem is you. But it's not. It's the loss of emotional safety that warps your sense of self.

Learned Helplessness & the Fog of Control

There's a term called learned helplessness. It describes what happens when someone experiences repeated harm or control and comes to believe they have no power to change it.

You stop fighting. You freeze. You tolerate things you never thought you would, because hope feels more dangerous than staying stuck. Often, this is when people start to notice physical symptoms of the abuse. I let everything go and just lay there. While I used to love to cook for my family, now I would make a box of mac and cheese or get fast food for days on end. Parenting became nearly obsolete as I would float, completely traumatized, through important moments. I remember one day in particular, I spilled a glass of water while lying in bed. Before, I would have done what most people would have done: I would have gotten a towel to get it cleaned up, and I would have changed the sheets to ensure it didn't soak through to the mattress. Instead, I moved over to another part of the bed and just stared at the wall. I didn't have the energy to clean up a mess I was actually physically lying on. In my mind, what did it matter? Whether I cleaned the water, whether I cooked the elaborate dinner, it would never change my situation. So why even try?

If you find yourself feeling this way, it doesn't mean you're weak. It means your brain did what it had to do to survive.

Tools to Begin Reclaiming Yourself

Reconnecting with yourself after abuse is like slowly emerging from fog. You don't have to have all the answers; you just have to take small steps toward your truth.

1. Name What You've Been Through

Instead of minimizing, try saying it plainly:

"I've experienced emotional abuse."

"I've lived in a trauma response for a long time."

"What happened to me was not okay."

Naming it is powerful. It breaks the silence inside you. You don't have to say it to anyone else yet—just say it to yourself. Write it down. Speak it out loud in an empty room.

The truth doesn't need witnesses to be true.

2. Start with "Small Truths."

Ask yourself: What do I like? What do I want? What do I feel?

These may seem like small questions, but they're acts of rebellion when you've been controlled.

Your preferences matter. Your desires matter. Your feelings matter—even if someone spent years telling you they didn't.

Identity Reclamation Questions:

Start here. You don't need to answer all of these at once. Pick one. Sit with it. Let the answer come slowly.

"Before this relationship, what did I enjoy doing?"

Not what you were good at or what impressed people—what brought you joy? What made you lose track of time? What did you do just because you wanted to?

"What would I choose if no one were judging me?"

If there were no consequences, no one's opinion to manage, no punishment for choosing wrong, what would you pick? Where would you go? What would you wear? What would you say?

"What did people used to say they liked about me?"

Go back before the relationship, before the criticism and the put-downs. What did friends appreciate about you? What did you receive compliments on? Who were you when you felt free?

3. *Notice Emotional Flashbacks—and Learn to Ground Yourself*

If you feel panicked, ashamed, or enraged "for no reason," pause. You might be reacting to past fear, not present danger.

Emotional flashbacks are one of the cruelest symptoms of CPTSD because they feel like they're happening now, even when the threat is gone. Your body doesn't know the difference between a memory and a current crisis.

When you feel yourself spiraling, try these grounding techniques:

- Say it out loud:

"This is a memory, not what is happening right now."

"I am safe now. This feeling is real, but the danger is not."

"My body is reacting to the past. I am not in that place anymore."

Your voice is an anchor. Hearing yourself say it helps your brain register that you're here, not there.

- The 5-4-3-2-1 Technique

This pulls you out of your head and back into the present moment by engaging your senses.

Name 5 things you can see.

Look around the room. A lamp. A book. Your hands. The corner of a table. A shadow on the wall. Say them out loud or in your head.

Name 4 things you can hear.

The hum of the refrigerator. A car passing outside. Your own breathing. A clock ticking. Focus on the sounds happening right now.

Name 3 things you can physically touch.

Press your feet into the floor. Run your hand over the fabric of your shirt. Touch the table in front of you. Feel the texture. Notice the temperature.

Name 2 things you can smell.

If nothing is obvious, smell your sleeve, your coffee, the air. Even noticing that you can't smell anything grounds you in the moment.

Name 1 thing you can taste.

The lingering taste of toothpaste. Coffee. Water. Your own mouth. It doesn't matter what it is—just notice it.

This technique works because it forces your brain to process the present, not the past. Do it slowly. Let each sense have space.

You can do this anywhere. At your desk. In a meeting. In your car. No one will notice, but your nervous system will.

4. Practice Self-Compassion (Especially When You're Being Hard on Yourself)

This one is harder than it sounds. After years of being told you're the problem, it's easy to continue that internal narrative on your own.

But here's the truth: You are doing the best you can in an impossible situation. You deserve kindness—especially from yourself.

When you catch yourself thinking:

"I'm so weak."

"I should have left sooner."

"Why can't I just get over this?"

"I'm a bad mother/partner/employee/person."

Stop. And say this instead:

"I am doing the best I can in an impossible situation."

"I deserve kindness, especially from myself."

"I survived. That took strength, not weakness."

You wouldn't speak to a friend the way you speak to yourself. You wouldn't tell a survivor of abuse that they're pathetic for struggling to recover. So why do you say it to yourself?

Self-compassion isn't indulgence. It's not letting yourself off the hook. It's recognizing that you've been through something brutal, and you're still here. That deserves gentleness, not more cruelty.

5. Find an Experienced Trauma Therapist

Finding someone I connected with and who was trained in trauma recovery was key to my recovery. At first, the process can be daunting, but once you find this person, you can really begin to dig down and heal.

Look for therapists trained in:

- EMDR (Eye Movement Desensitization and Reprocessing): Excellent for trauma processing
- Somatic therapy: Focuses on how trauma lives in the body
- Internal Family Systems (IFS): Helps you reconnect with different parts of yourself
- Trauma-Focused CBT: Reframes thought patterns shaped by abuse

Not every therapist will be the right fit. If the first one doesn't feel safe or doesn't understand complex trauma, keep looking. You deserve someone who gets it.

I cannot emphasize the importance of this step enough. You don't have to do this alone. And you shouldn't

Quick Chapter Summary

- CPTSD comes from long-term emotional abuse and control.
- Common symptoms include self-doubt, emotional numbness, and people-pleasing.
- Control slowly erodes your identity, and you begin to live in fear, not freedom.
- You are not broken. You adapted to survive. Healing is about remembering who you are.

Chapter 4
Knowing When It Is Time to Leave –
Listening to the Voice Inside

When determining if it is time to leave, it is common that we begin to think of excuses. At least he hasn't hit me. He had a hard childhood; it's not his fault. He is just under a lot of stress at work; he doesn't mean it. I used to tell myself, It's not that bad. But the truth was, I hadn't slept well in months, and my mental health was rapidly deteriorating. His negative energy produced a whirlwind that often left me confused as to what was even going on. My memory was horrible. My face was puffy from crying. One occasional glass of wine turned into a bottle; anything I could do to ease the mental pain, I was willing to try. I constantly tried to anticipate what mood he would be in so I could adjust. I smiled in front of others, but cried in silence every single night, not that he cared.

While I didn't wake up one morning with an epiphany that it was time to go, things were getting more dangerous in the household. Leaving presented so many very scary scenarios. Mostly around the safety of my teenage daughter. There were also the questions of where I would live, how I could afford it on my own, and what I would tell others. By that time, I was completely isolated. There was no more laughter in my life. I stopped reaching out to friends. I was languishing in a very chaotic, high-stress work environment, which only deepened my sense of trauma. My career was suffering, and bad. There was very little left of my former self.

But incredibly, even with all of this, it still was not enough. I believed in him, and I believed in the power of unconditional love. Divorce was highly discouraged in my religion, and I was taught that, aside from cheating, there was absolutely no excuse for it. This mindset proved to be very dangerous as it made me feel somehow at fault. I fixated on praying it all away. Meanwhile, I needed to run, now.

What makes people finally leave is different for everyone. For me, it was my child. I could not leave her without a mother if he did end up killing me one day. What scared me even more was that if she saw me pick a man like that, she might follow my example one day and pick someone like him. The thought that her life could be in danger here or in the future was more than I could bear. So, I decided to end the marriage.

If you're wondering if it's time to leave, that may be the sign you need that the answer is YES. You don't need to wait for a final straw. Leaving may be the scariest thing you've ever had to do. I encourage you to listen to the quiet voice that's been whispering: This isn't love. This isn't safe.

Why Is Leaving So Hard?

Abusers condition you to doubt your instincts.

They twist reality until you question your own memory, your own feelings. They drip-feed affection just enough to keep you hoping things will change. And that hope? It keeps you stuck. Just like an animal in the wild with primitive instincts, they seem to know somehow that you are getting fed up. This can cause them to straighten up just enough that you will keep trying.

But here's the truth:

If you're asking whether it's time to leave, something inside you already knows.

False Hope vs. Real Safety

Abuse cycles between harm and honeymoon.

You'll have horrible fights followed by moments of intense love, apologies, and promises to change. But if the cycle keeps repeating, if their kindness is conditional or rare, you are not in a safe relationship.

Hope is not a safety plan.

Hope says, "Maybe it will get better."

Reality asks, "What if it doesn't?"

Key Signs It Might Be Time to Leave

You don't need all of these to be true. One is enough.

- You're constantly walking on eggshells.
- Your mental or physical health is suffering.
- You've lost interest in the things you once enjoyed.

- You feel afraid. Not just during fights, but all the time.
- You're isolated from people who care about you.
- You feel like you're "crazy" or overly emotional.
- You find yourself making excuses for their behavior. Again.
- You fantasize about leaving, or disappearing altogether.

If any of these resonate, you are not overreacting. You are waking up.

What If It Isn't Physical?

Many survivors stay because the abuse "wasn't that bad" or "never got physical."

But emotional, verbal, and psychological abuse can be just as damaging, sometimes even more so, because it's harder to see. The vast majority of my abuse was not physical. However, does it have to be? Out of control people are, by definition, out of control. Who knows what they will do?

If it's destroying your peace, it's destroying your life.

No one gets to decide what's "bad enough" except you.

What If It is Physical?

This is going to be the shortest section of this book. If it is physical, there is no other choice for you but to leave. In these instances, I highly encourage you to seek outside resources. DO NOT KEEP IT TO YOURSELF. This is a time to use your voice. Once our lives are at stake, the conversation is over. Be smart, be clever enough to keep them calm, but meanwhile make a plan, and GO.

Fear Is Not a Reason to Stay

Fear of the unknown is valid.

Fear of being alone, starting over, being judged, or not being believed, it's all real. But staying out of fear is not the same as staying because you're safe or loved.

If you're terrified of how they'll react when you say, "I'm leaving," that's not love.

That's a warning.

The Moment You Realize: Enough Is Enough

Your breaking point doesn't have to be dramatic.

It might be a cruel word they throw at you in front of your child.

It might be realizing your body has been in fight-or-flight mode for months.

It might just be looking at yourself in the mirror and whispering, I deserve more than this.

Leaving doesn't mean you stopped loving them.

It means you started loving yourself.

Practical Clarity Check: 5 Questions to Ask Yourself

1. Do I feel safe, physically, emotionally, mentally around them?
2. Am I still allowed to have boundaries, privacy, or opinions?
3. Is the relationship healing me or harming me?
4. Do I feel more myself or less myself with them?
5. If my child or best friend were in this same situation, what would I want for them?

Your answers will tell you more than their words ever will.

1. Quick Tools to Help You Get Clear

"If I Were Free" Visualization

Close your eyes and imagine a life where you feel:

- Calm
- Safe
- Not afraid of being yelled at, hurt, or manipulated

Write down how your body feels in that moment. That's your compass.

2. "The Scale" Exercise

On a scale from 1 to 10, how safe do you feel in this relationship?

How exhausted? How happy?

Repeat this weekly and notice the pattern. Numbers don't lie.

3. Emergency Clarity List

Create two columns:

- Left: "Reasons I want to stay."
- Right: "What's actually happening day-to-day."

Seeing it on paper often helps break the illusion of the relationship you wish you had.

4. Write a Letter to Your Future Self

This one is powerful, and I wish I had done it sooner. When you're in the thick of it — when you're scared, when you're doubting yourself, when the fear of leaving feels bigger than the fear of staying — it's easy to forget why you wanted out in the first place. So write it down. Right now. While it's fresh. While you still remember how bad it really is.

Instructions: Find a quiet moment. Open a notes app on your phone, grab a journal, or type it into a password-protected document. Write a letter to the version of yourself who might waver. The version that might be considered going back to. The version that might forget. Start with:

"Dear [Your Name], I'm writing this to you on [today's date] because I need you to remember…" Then answer these questions honestly:

What happened that made you realize it was time to leave?

Not the whole history—just the moment (or moments) that broke you. The thing that made you say "enough."

How do you feel right now, living in this relationship?

Describe it. The fear. The exhaustion. The constant walking on eggshells. The version of yourself you've become. Don't sugarcoat it.

What are you afraid will happen if you stay?

To you. To your kids. To your health, your sanity, your life.

What do you want your future to look like?

Not necessarily the details—just the feeling. Peace. Safety. Freedom. The ability to breathe without waiting for the next explosion.

End with:

"If you're reading this and thinking about going back, please remember: You wrote this for a reason. You deserve better. Don't let fear convince you otherwise. I love you. Stay strong." Then save it somewhere safe. A folder on your phone. An email draft. A note hidden in a book. And when the doubt creeps in—when they're being nice again, when you're second-guessing yourself, when you feel weak—pull it out and read it. Let the version of you who was still IN it remind the version of you who's trying to get OUT why you can't go back.

5. Create Your "What I Deserve" List

This exercise is simple, but it's a gut-check. When you've been in an abusive relationship for a long time, your standards erode. You start accepting things that would have horrified you years ago. You forget what normal, healthy, safe love actually looks like. So let's reset the baseline.

Instructions: Make two columns. Do this on paper, in your phone, wherever you can be honest. Column 1: What Every Person Deserves in a Relationship: Write down the absolute basics — the things that should be non-negotiable for everyone. Not "nice to haves." Just the foundational, baseline respect every human being deserves from a partner. Here's a starting list (add your own):

✓ To feel physically safe

✓ To feel emotionally safe

✓ To have my feelings acknowledged and respected

✓ To be spoken to with kindness, even during conflict

✓ To have privacy and personal boundaries

✓ To make decisions about my own body, time, and life

✓ To see friends and family without needing permission

✓ To have my needs matter, not just theirs

✓ To be trusted, not monitored or accused constantly

✓ To make mistakes without being torn apart for them

✓ To have bad days without being attacked for them

✓ To be loved for who I am, not controlled into who they want me to be

Add anything else that feels essential to you. What would you want for your daughter? Your best friend? Your younger self? Write those down too.

Column 2: What I'm Actually Getting: Now go through that list, one by one. Put a check mark next to every item you're actually experiencing in your current relationship. Be brutally honest. Then put an X next to everything you're not getting—or that's actively being violated. Now look at your list. How many checkmarks do you have?

How many X's? If your list is mostly X's—or if even one of those foundational needs (like physical safety, emotional safety, or having your feelings matter) has an X next to it—you have your answer. You're not asking for too much. You're asking for the bare minimum.

Quick Chapter Summary

- If you're wondering if it's time to leave, you're already hearing the truth inside.
- Abuse isn't always visible—but the damage is real.
- Hope without change is just a delay.

- Fear is valid—but not a reason to stay.
- You don't need more proof. You just need peace.
- Listen to your body. It already knows what your mind is trying to explain away.

Chapter 5
Staying Safe While You're Inside

The day I realized I needed to leave, I also realized I couldn't, not yet.

He always had an uncanny way of knowing. For me, his favorite type of abuse was one of neglect. His main strategy was to make me feel as if all my love, my value as a woman, was insignificant to him. For him, he made it clear that, although I was his wife, I was not valued or loved. If I left, good for him. I was nothing. And this hurt me in a way I could not explain.

This type of abuse, one of neglect, led me to the false knowledge that the best I could ever give a man was not enough. I was less than a human to him. I felt sick, disgusting, and dumb. All of the things he told me, I absorbed like a sponge. Although this was extremely abusive and damaging, his particular flavor was more based on quiet control and cruelty in his words.

He made it clear that I was disgusting to him now, my value, less than nothing. He made it clear that once I left, he would start his life over with a "normal" woman, one with value who didn't have all of these problems I had. One who wasn't crazy, out of control, and always sad.

↘ All of my efforts to show him my love and value had not been enough. Ultimately, by this point, I believed I was not a worthy person. I had tried to do better, but by then I realized that wasn't what he wanted. He wanted control and a reason to leave.

Terror began to set in as I realized that even though all his love for me was gone, he had also burned all bridges. He had nothing to lose. This made him unafraid to hit, to threaten, to terrify. Someone who feels they have nothing to lose is in a very dangerous situation. DO NOT TEST THE WATERS.

As I made my decision, other questions mounted. Where would I even go? I would need to find an apartment, which meant a large security deposit. My daughter had managed to feel some stability in school, even when her home life was unstable. This could make it worse. I thought about our families. Leaving required me to "come out" in a certain way. I had to admit the dream was over. Besides, I loved my home. I had nowhere to take my pets. The challenges mounted. However, one day after a particularly nasty fight, I told him to leave. With every bit of strength I could muster, I screamed it, LEAVE NOW.

At the end of the day, he did leave that night and never returned. Although there would be many harrowing months ahead in the divorce process, he was physically gone. I quickly discovered an affair that made that transition easy for him. At the time, I didn't realize it, but in retrospect, the signs were all there.

Oddly, I was still heartbroken. I now know that it was a trauma bond. I had become so accustomed to living my life in fight or flight that was all I knew. Although he could kill me one day, everything in me screamed to go back. It took a lot of self-talk to remind myself why I could not go back. I wrote those reasons down and repeated them over and over again. Each day I hung on, just to struggle again the next. The weeks went by, and I stayed on autopilot. Somehow, I got myself to a lawyer and filed divorce paperwork. Eventually, the decision got easier.

Ultimately, the divorce was scary. Very scary. I made it safely to divorce day through restraint and cleverness. I carefully calculated what battles to fight and which ones to let go. There were times I gave him much more kindness than he deserved. It was a lot to navigate, but ultimately, with violent people, it is better to lose an argument by letting them be "right" than proving a point.

In fact, allowing him to be "right" could save your life. Prove your "rightness" to someone else. It is his image wants to protect. Holding a mirror up to his behavior can often lead to a thought process that looks something like, if I am never going to be a good person, then I might as well commit a violent act. This is very dangerous.

I felt like I was walking a tightrope, every move a possible trigger. I knew that one wrong word, one flicker of truth in my eyes, and the consequences could be immediate and dangerous.

I have learned that in one way or another, for whatever reason, they are always watching everything. Your behavior, your habits, your tone—usually, through social media and emails. Whether they are dismissive or clingy, never assume that they are not watching and calculating. Keep this in mind.

To survive, I started to play a part. Not forever, just long enough to gather what I needed to safely leave. I smiled when I needed to. I responded the way he expected. And inside, I was building my exit—quietly, intentionally, safely.

If you're in that stage, this is your chapter. You are not weak for staying. You are being strategic. You are surviving. And soon, you will escape.

Why Safety Planning Matters Before You Leave?

Leaving an abusive relationship can be the most dangerous time.

Abusers lose control—and that's what scares them most. That's when they lash out.

Leaving is not about proving to them that they are wrong. They will never believe they are wrong. If they were capable of this, they wouldn't be an unsafe person. Remember, you are smarter than them, you are cleverer. You can do it with planning. Here is what worked for me.

Stay Calm on the Outside, Clear on the Inside

When you're still living under their roof (or in contact daily), your number one goal is safety and stability. This means:

- Keeping your real thoughts and plans to yourself
- Avoiding unnecessary arguments
- Playing along when needed to avoid escalation

You are not betraying yourself by doing this. You are keeping yourself safe.

Survival is not weakness. It's wisdom.

Safety Tips While You're Still There

1. Don't Announce Your Plans

Never tell your abuser you're thinking of leaving. Even in a moment of anger.

If they sense distance or rebellion, they may increase control, surveillance, or violence.

2. Use the "Notebook" Technique

Keep a hidden notebook (physical or digital) with:

- Instances of abuse (dates, what happened)
- Copies of important documents or numbers
- Names of trusted people who know the truth

Hide it somewhere secure—away from their access. Or use code names and email it to a friend under a decoy subject line.

3. Prepare Essentials Slowly

Start gathering:

- Copies of IDs, birth certificates, and social security cards
- Emergency money (cash if possible)
- A backup phone (or an old one with Wi-Fi only)
- A safe place to go, even temporarily

Stash them somewhere safe—a friend's home, your car, a locker, or with a coworker.

4. Control Your Digital Trail

- Clear search history often
- Use incognito mode or a separate browser
- Don't store passwords in your phone
- Use a secret email address for planning

If you suspect your phone is being monitored, try using a public device to research or call for help.

5. Create a Code Word

Pick a word or phrase that signals danger. Share it with a trusted friend or family member.

Example: "Can you bring the blue sweater?" could mean "Call 911 for me."

6. Watch Your Reactions

Try not to act "different" if you're preparing to leave. Abusers notice subtle shifts:

- Don't withdraw too quickly
- Avoid suddenly standing up for yourself if you haven't before
- Stay in the role until it's safe to exit

You are playing a role—not because you're fake, but because your real self deserves to survive.

7. Practice Emergency Scenarios

If things escalate suddenly:

- Know at least two exits from your home or building
- Identify safe rooms with locks and no weapons (bathroom > kitchen)
- Keep your car fueled and parked facing out, if possible
- Keep shoes and keys near the door, just in case

This isn't paranoia. It's preparation.

8. Seek Professional Help

Some experienced individuals have had extensive exposure to these types of situations. They will be able to advise you of the best strategy to leave safely. You must involve outside help.

With that being said, if it is urgent, if you suspect things might be getting dangerous. By all means, GO and call the police immediately.

Small Acts of Autonomy (While You're Still Inside)

Reclaiming Pieces of Yourself in Secret

When you're still living with an abuser, survival often means shrinking yourself. Playing small. Staying quiet. Doing whatever keeps the peace.

But here's what I learned: even in captivity, you can practice tiny acts of freedom.

These aren't big, dramatic gestures. They're small, quiet, invisible ways to remind yourself that you still exist. That you're still a person with preferences, desires, and autonomy — even if no one else sees it yet.

These acts won't fix the situation. But they will keep a part of you alive until you can get out.

These small acts are designed to be invisible, safe, and completely under your control. Pick one. Try it. Let it be yours.

1. *Choose something small, just for yourself*

Pick one thing—no matter how tiny—that is your choice alone.

Examples:

Order your coffee exactly how you like it, even if he makes fun of your order

Take a different route to work, just because you want to see something new

Listen to a song he hates when you're alone in the car

Why this works: It reminds your brain that you still have agency. You can still make choices, even if they're invisible to everyone else.

These aren't acts of rebellion designed to provoke him. They're acts of self-preservation designed to keep you intact.

2. *Reconnect with one trusted person, even just by text*

Isolation is one of the abuser's most powerful tools. The more cut off you are, the harder it is to leave.

But reconnection doesn't have to be dramatic. You don't need to confess everything. You don't need to explain why you disappeared. Just send one text to one person you trust.

Safety note: If your phone is monitored, be strategic. Use a friend's phone. Create a new email or social media account he doesn't know about. Or wait until you're somewhere he can't see your screen.

3. Take a short walk alone to clear your head

If you can, take 10 minutes by yourself.

Walk around the block. Sit in your car in a parking lot. Stand outside and breathe.

No agenda. No destination. Just the time that belongs to you.

Why this works: It breaks the suffocating cycle of hypervigilance. Even a few minutes of physical distance can help your nervous system regulate. You're not running away—you're just stepping outside his immediate control for a breath.

4. Keep one small thing that is just yours

Find something—anything—that he doesn't control, doesn't know about, or can't take away.

Examples:

A journal hidden in your car or at work (even if you only write one sentence a week)

A playlist saved under a generic name that no one else would recognize

A photo on your phone that reminds you of who you were before him

A small amount of cash tucked somewhere he'll never look

Why this works: It's proof that not everything in your life belongs to him. This thing—this tiny, hidden thing—is yours. And when you leave, it will come with you.

It might seem silly. A hidden $20 bill. A secret playlist. But these things are anchors. They remind you that you still exist as a separate person, even when everything else feels like it's been absorbed into his control.

Quick Chapter Summary

- The time before you leave is when risk is highest. Stay calm and strategic.
- Don't share your plans. Don't provoke unnecessary conflict.
- Gather documents, cash, and contacts quietly.
- Protect your digital privacy and emotional energy.
- Survival mode is not a weakness. It's how you'll stay alive long enough to break free.

Chapter 6
Leaving Safely – Planning and Executing Your Exit

It's no secret that leaving is the most dangerous part of your journey to freedom. Just turn on the news.

Leaving is rarely a simple, clean break. And probably most importantly, it may not feel good at first. Expect that. The relief comes later, and it may be many months, if not years, to feel truly safe again in your body.

Leaving can look many ways. It's important not to compare your story with others. Just like we are all unique people, each story will also be unique. Some feel a sense of relief; they walk away feeling free, like the world is finally theirs to take. Others feel scared, heartbroken, unsure. All of the things. Just know that it's okay to feel those things. However, it does not change the reality of the situation. It is not safe.

To be honest, the day my husband left, I was so exhausted that I felt nothing at all. I had no energy and very little fight left in me. It reminded me of a war movie where the hero crawls on the ground to safety just to use their last breaths to say a dramatic goodbye. The only thing that gave me that motivation to crawl to safety was simple: I did not want to die. I knew without a doubt that one day he would go too far. My inner dialogue was telling me that he would never do such a thing. While emotionally abusive and sometimes violent, he had never punched me, right? So, he wouldn't end my life.

The truth was, even if he did not necessarily "mean to do it," he was an unsafe person. He was completely out of control, impulsive, and angry. His hands around my neck could linger just 30 seconds too long, and at the end of those 30 seconds, all that I had gone through from birth until that day was in vain. I would no longer be on this earth. And my child, motherless. I did not want to die!

For some, leaving is a straightforward decision. They decide to leave, and they go. For others, the path is winding and long. There isn't a specific day when you walk out, close the door behind you, and never return. For some, you may have nowhere to go when you walk out. There are extenuating factors. Kids, animals you cannot leave behind.

However, you feel, if you have made it this far, I believe that you are close. You're preparing, planning, or just dreaming of the way out. Take a breath. You're not alone. And you're about to do something deeply courageous.

Why Leaving Is So Dangerous (and So Brave)

Let's start with what no one likes to say out loud: leaving an abusive relationship is the most dangerous part. The moment someone with control issues senses they're losing power, they escalate. They might cry, rage, beg, stalk, sabotage, or threaten. Not because they love you, but because you were never supposed to leave.

Please listen very closely when I say this: crying, raging, stalking, sabotage, and threats are NOT love. If you start believing that, stop yourself now. Be brutally honest with yourself. Pain is not love. Believe me, it will feel good for a moment when you see that glimpse of who they used to be. They show a glimpse of a definite purpose: to bring you back to the trap.

And what is a trap? It offers something attractive that draws you in. Then BAM, you are caught again. Love does not look like crying every day, it doesn't look like confusion, it is not physical. Think about it. It would horrify you to treat a loved one this way. You would become aware of what you did wrong and genuinely feel bad. Then you would do your best to change.

That's why this chapter isn't about dramatic ultimatums. It's about a quiet strategy. It's about getting you out in one piece, with your sanity intact. And it starts before the door ever closes behind you.

Leaving Isn't Just an Act — It's a Process

Leaving an abusive relationship isn't one single moment. It's a sequence of decisions that all prioritize your safety and your future.

It doesn't need to be perfect. It doesn't need to make sense to anyone else. It just needs to keep you alive, stable, and free.

This chapter will walk you through what to do, what to bring, who to call, and how to protect yourself, step by step.

Resource Information

You Don't Have to Do This Alone

Before we go any further, I need you to know something: there are people whose entire job is to help you leave safely.

You don't need to figure this out on your own. You don't need to have all the answers. You just need to reach out.

They can help you:

- Create a personalized safety plan
- Find local shelters and resources
- Connect with legal advocates
- Talk through your options without judgment
- Get emergency help if you're in immediate danger

You don't need to have your story perfectly organized. You don't need to justify why you're calling. You just need to pick up the phone.

If your phone is monitored or you're worried about your call history:

- Use a friend's phone
- Call from work on a break
- Use a public phone (gas stations, libraries, some stores still have them)
- Use the online chat feature at TheHotline.org from a safe device

Safe Computer Access

If you need to research shelters, legal options, or escape plans but don't have a safe device at home:

Public libraries offer private computer access.

Most libraries:

- Have computers available for free public use
- Allow you to browse without logging in with personal information
- Offer privacy (you can request a computer in a corner or away from foot traffic)
- Have staff who won't ask questions or report what you're searching for

Library computers are ideal for:

- Looking up domestic violence resources
- Finding shelters or safe housing
- Contacting advocates via email or online chat
- Researching legal options or reading about leaving safely

Important: Clear your browsing history when you're done, or use incognito/private browsing mode. If you're unsure how, ask a librarian—they've helped people in your situation before, and they won't judge you.

You Are Not Alone

Millions of people have left abusive relationships. Many of them had no plan, no money, and no idea where they were going.

But they left. And they survived. And so, will you.

The hotline, the shelters, the advocates—they exist because people like you need help. And asking for help isn't a weakness. It's the smartest, bravest thing you can do.

What to Do Before You Leave

This assumes you've already started safety planning (see Chapter 5), and now you're ready to act.

1. Choose a Safe Day and Time

- Weekday mornings are often safer, less suspicious, and have more people around.
- Avoid holidays or emotionally loaded days when tensions may be higher.
- Leave when the abuser is away at work, running errands, or distracted.

2. Know Where You're Going

You need a safe, prearranged destination. Options include:

- A trusted friend or family member's house (only if safe and unknown to the abuser)
- A domestic violence shelter (confidential and often 24/7)

- A hotel or temporary rental using a prepaid card or safe account

Tip: Don't go to a place the abuser knows or has access to. And don't post your location online.

3. Pack an Emergency Bag

If you can't pack ahead of time, do it quickly the day of. Essentials include:

- Photo ID, birth certificate, Social Security card
- Phone charger, burner phone (if possible)
- Medications
- Some cash and/or a prepaid debit card
- A change of clothes, keys, and essential toiletries
- Copies of any restraining orders or custody documents (if you already have them)

Leave this bag somewhere safe before your exit day or have someone bring it to you once you're safe.

4. Inform Someone You Trust

Let someone reliable know your plan. Give them:

- Your timeline
- Your backup plan (if something goes wrong)
- A code word for danger ("If I say ____, call 911")

If no one safe is available, call a domestic violence hotline for help creating a secure plan.

How to Leave in the Moment

1. Keep It Simple

Don't explain. Don't argue. Don't announce.

Just go. Calmly. Quietly. Safely.

If confrontation is unavoidable:

- Have a reason that won't provoke suspicion (errands, appointment, etc.)
- Keep your tone flat and unthreatening
- Say what's necessary, but keep moving

2. Leave All Communication Devices Behind If Needed

If you think your phone is monitored, leave it behind. Get to safety first, then use a clean phone or public line.

3. Go Straight to Safety

Don't make extra stops. Don't go back "just one more time."

Abusers often escalate right after you leave. Prioritize disappearing, not finishing.

After You Leave: Protecting Your Freedom

1. Block and Cut Contact

- Change your number or get a new phone
- Block them on social media, and set all accounts to private
- Ask friends not to share your updates or location

2. Consider a Restraining Order

Depending on your situation, this can:

- Prohibit contact, even through others
- Grant you sole use of your home (in some cases)
- Help with custody or legal protection

Consult a legal advocate or domestic violence agency before filing.

3. Secure Your Privacy

- Update passwords (email, bank, insurance)
- Freeze your credit, if needed
- Use new logins for everything, even Netflix
- Stop location sharing on all apps (including shared family plans)

What If You Have Kids?

This complicates things, but it's not impossible.

- Bring all custody/legal documents you have
- Talk to a lawyer or advocate ahead of time if you can
- Do not violate any custody orders without legal advice—it could backfire

Many states have protective measures to help you leave safely with children. You don't have to navigate it alone.

Most importantly, check in with them about how they are feeling. Although they are smaller than us, they still have little nervous systems that are also processing deeply traumatic experiences. It is very important to monitor them for signs of stress and seek professional help for them as quickly as possible.

Permission to Leave Imperfectly

I need to tell you something that no one else might say:

You do not need to have everything figured out.

You don't need the perfect plan. You don't need six months' rent saved. You don't need a new job lined up, a therapist in place, or a flawless exit strategy.

You just need to be safer than you are right now.

That's it. That's the bar.

Leaving imperfectly is still leaving.

Maybe you only grab half the things you meant to pack.

Maybe you leave in the middle of the night with nothing but your keys and your phone.

Maybe you go to a shelter instead of a friend's house because it's the only option.

Maybe you don't have custody paperwork, or a restraining order, or proof of abuse.

Maybe you're leaving with debt, with no savings, with nowhere to go but anywhere but here.

That's okay. You're still doing it.

Progress, not perfection.

You don't need permission to leave—but I'm giving it to you anyway.

You don't need to wait until:

He hits you 'hard enough' to justify it

You have enough money saved

Your kids are older

You've tried therapy one more time

You've given him "one more chance."

You can leave now. Messy. Imperfect. Scared. Uncertain.

You can leave and figure the rest out later.

Because staying in danger while you wait for the perfect moment to leave is not safer. It's just more time for things to get worse.

Your life doesn't have to be perfectly rebuilt to be worth saving.

Leaving is not the end of hard things. It's the beginning of different hard things — ones that don't involve living in fear.

You don't need a savings account, a support system, a job offer, or a picture-perfect Plan B.

You need out. And out is enough.

Everything else? You'll figure it out. One day at a time. One decision at a time. One breath at a time.

But first, you have to leave.

So, leave. However, you can. Whenever you can.

And trust that the version of you who's free — even broke, even scared, even starting from scratch — is still better off than the version of you who stayed.

You've got this. And I'm rooting for you.

Quick Chapter Summary

- Leaving safely means planning, preparing, and staying calm.
- Choose a time when you're least likely to be stopped.
- Bring essentials, go straight to your safe space, and cut contact.
- Secure your digital and physical safety.
- Get help with legal and custody concerns—you're not alone

Chapter 7
You Made It Out – Now What?

The weeks and months after the end of an abusive relationship are very emotional and require lots of self-love. After the end of my marriage, I recognized in the immediate days after how much my nervous system had been damaged. I must admit that for me, the first feelings I had were not of relief, they were of intense sadness. It is very easy to get confused about your own story. Remember the survival instincts that helped you to leave will help you make it through this as well.

You've Survived—That's Not Small

Take a moment to realize what you've already done:

- You faced a truth that many people ignore
- You broke through manipulation and confusion
- You made a plan, trusted yourself, and followed through
- You chose safety over familiarity

That's powerful. That's brave. That's enough for today.

The First Week: Just Get Through It

The first days and weeks after leaving are survival mode. You're not supposed to have it all figured out. You're not supposed to feel good yet. You're just supposed to get through. Here's what helped me—and what might help you:

1.Take care of your body (even when you don't want to):

Your nervous system has been in overdrive for months, maybe years. Now that the immediate threat is gone, your body might crash. Do these things, even if they feel impossible:

Drink water. Set a timer if you have to. Dehydration makes anxiety worse, and you're probably already dehydrated from stress.

Eat something. Anything. A granola bar. Toast. Crackers. You don't need a full meal, just fuel. Your brain can't function without it.

Sleep when you can. If you can't sleep, rest. Lie down. Close your eyes. Your body needs permission to stop running.

If someone offers to bring you food, let them. If you can't eat, don't force it—but keep trying. Small bites. One thing at a time. Your body kept you alive through hell. Honor it by keeping it fed, hydrated, and rested—even minimally.

2. Do not make any big decisions right away:

You just made the biggest decision of your life. You left. That's enough for now.

Don't:

- Quit your job
- Move to a new city (unless it's part of your safety plan)

- Cut off your entire support system
- Make major financial commitments
- Start dating
- Commit to long-term plans you're not ready for

Your brain is still in crisis mode. You're running on adrenaline, fear, relief, grief—all at once. That's not the time to make decisions that will affect the next year of your life. Let your nervous system start to regulate. Then reassess. Right now? Just focus on today. Sometimes just the next hour.

3. Let yourself feel whatever comes:

You might cry for hours.

You might feel nothing at all.

You might be furious one minute and heartbroken the next.

You might laugh at something stupid and then feel guilty for laughing.

You might miss him, even though you know you can't go back.

All of it is normal. All of it is allowed. There's no 'right' way to feel after leaving. You don't need to perform relief, gratitude, or strength for anyone—including yourself.

4. Reach out to one safe person:

You don't need to tell everyone. You don't need to explain everything. You don't even need to have a full conversation. But if you can, tell one person you trust. Text them:

"I left. I'm safe. I'm not ready to talk yet, but I wanted you to know."

Isolation was part of the abuse. Reaching out—even minimally—starts to break that pattern. It reminds you that you're not alone. That someone knows. That someone cares. And if you don't have a safe person? Call the National Domestic Violence Hotline (1-800-799-7233). They're there for this exact moment. You don't need a crisis to call—you can call just to say you left and you're scared, and you don't know what to do next. They'll listen. They won't judge. And they'll help you figure out the next step.

5. Do one small thing that's just for you:

This sounds silly when you're in survival mode, but it matters. Pick one tiny thing that brings you even a flicker of comfort:

- Make your favorite coffee or tea
- Take a long shower without rushing
- Watch a show you actually want to watch (not one he chose)
- Sit outside for five minutes and just breathe

This isn't about self-care. It's about reminding your brain that you're allowed to have preferences again. That your comfort matters. That you're safe enough now to want something small and claim it. It won't fix everything. But it's a start.

What Comes Next Isn't a Race — It's a Rebuilding

You might feel:

- Relieved and still afraid
- Free and wildly lost
- Numb, confused, or suddenly overwhelmed

All of that is normal. You're not broken. You're adjusting to a life you weren't allowed to imagine for a long time.

What comes next might include:

- Grieving what was supposed to be
- Unlearning the lies you were told about yourself
- Remembering who you are underneath the trauma
- Feeling lonely, even though you're safer than ever

It's okay to take it slow. Safety is the foundation. Healing is the journey.

You Don't Owe Anyone Your Story

You may feel pressure to explain what happened — to friends, family, even yourself.

You don't have to. You can share when and how you're ready. You can also say:

- "I left a painful situation."
- "I'm focusing on my healing."
- "I'm not ready to talk about it, but thank you for asking."

Surviving is not a show for anyone else. It's your truth. You're allowed to protect it.

Some final thoughts that I want to share with you: there is no playbook for recovery. People will have lots of opinions. There are often family members and friends of theirs who will get involved. Unfortunately, they may not see your side. It is important to keep in mind that these same people have often contributed to the dysfunction that made them the unsafe person they are today. You will also have well-meaning friends and family with lots of pity as people learn what happened to you. All these people will have opinions. Some will also have judgment. One of the hardest comments I heard in the days after was, "I would never let that happen to me." These comments left me devastated. How had I let this happen to me? I thought I was strong.

When those thoughts come up, remind yourself deep inside your heart that you were scammed. You were sold a dream that nobody could ever resist. Over time, your body went into survival mode. When our bodies are in survival mode, some of the more advanced parts of the brain, the parts that make rational decisions and motivate us, shut down. It shuts down to save itself. When you are in an unsafe relationship, it is not the same as when your mind is at peak performance. You did what you could. Be gentle on yourself.

Even today, many years later, I am often reminded to give myself grace as my nervous system learns to be safe. There are times when something easy is too much. These things that don't always make sense to others. Recently, I was shopping at a large warehouse store. A few steps into "the experience" of the store, I was in a full-blown panic. It was crowded and chaotic, and the myriad of choices was overwhelming. Although I was physically safe, my body couldn't tell. I could not remember one thing that I came to buy. I pulled up my list, quickly walked through the store to grab some of the items I needed, and essentially fled the store as if it were on fire. I sat in my car after with my heart racing and just cried. Years later, and I was still fighting these battles. I have to admit it was hard. I tell this story to bring home the point that the emotional safety you need will not always make sense to others. Sometimes it won't even make sense in your own mind. Don't ever allow someone to shame you, not even yourself.

Ultimately, your story does not end magically the day you leave, but it does make you one thing. A survivor. Freedom is the beginning, not the end. You've done the hardest part. You've chosen yourself. You made the impossible possible.

And now… there's life after survival. It's waiting for you. One day at a time.

Resources for Support and Help

If you or someone you know is experiencing domestic violence, abuse, or mental health crisis, the following organizations and hotlines can provide confidential support, guidance, and resources.

---

988 Suicide & Crisis Lifeline – Call or text 988 for immediate support for mental health crises, including survivors of domestic violence. Available 24/7, confidential, and free.
Website: https://988lifeline.org

National Domestic Violence Hotline – Call 1-800-799-SAFE (7233) or text **START** to 88788 for confidential support, safety planning, and referral to local services. Available 24/7.
Website: https://www.thehotline.org

National Sexual Assault Hotline (RAINN) – Call 1-800-656-HOPE (4673) for support and resources for survivors of sexual assault.
Website: https://www.rainn.org

Crisis Text Line – Text HOME to 741741 to connect with trained crisis counselors via text, available 24/7.
Website: https://www.crisistextline.org

SAMHSA Helpline (Substance Abuse & Mental Health) – Call 1-800-662-4357 for confidential guidance, referrals, and support for mental health or substance use issues.
Website: https://www.samhsa.gov/find-help/national-helpline

Legal & Advocacy Support

Futures Without Violence – Provides legal information, safety planning tools, and advocacy programs for survivors.
Website: https://www.futureswithoutviolence.org

National Coalition Against Domestic Violence (NCADV) – Offers advocacy, education, and community support for survivors.
Website: https://www.ncadv.org

Legal Aid & Domestic Violence Clinics – Many states have specialized legal services for survivors.
Website: https://www.lsc.gov

Support for Children & Teens

Childhelp National Child Abuse Hotline – Call **1-800-422-4453** for help and guidance for children experiencing abuse.
Website: https://www.childhelp.org

Loveisrespect (Teen Dating Abuse Helpline) – Call **1-866-331-9474** or **Text LOVEIS to 22522** for confidential teen support and advocacy.
Website: https://www.loveisrespect.org

State & Local Resources

- To find local domestic violence programs and shelters in your state, visit: https://www.thehotline.org/find-help

- Local mental health agencies may also provide **988 access, counseling, and domestic violence support.**